RUBBER

Jacqueline Dineen

ENSLOW PUBLISHERS, INC.
Bloy St & Ramsey Ave.
Box 777
Hillside, N.J. 07205

Rubber is waterproof, stretchy, and strong. Here is the story of how this amazing material is grown and put to use.

Contents

The picture above shows formers for the moulding of rubber gloves.
[cover] The picture on the cover illustrates the best known use of rubber—car tyres.
[title page] The colourful balloons in the picture on the title page are made from liquid rubber.
[1—24] All other pictures are identified by number in the text.

This series was developed for a worldwide market.

First American Edition, 1988

Printed in the United States of America

10 9 8 7 6 5 4 3 2 1

LIBRARY OF CONGRESS
Library of Congress Cataloging-in-Publication Data

Dineen, Jacqueline.
    Rubber / Jacqueline Dineen.
        p.   cm. -- (The world's harvest)
    Includes index.
    Summary: Explains how rubber is grown and processed into useful objects.
    ISBN 0-89490-222-9
    1. Rubber--Juvenile literature. [1. Rubber.] I. Title.
II. Series: Dineen, Jacqueline. World's harvest.
TS1890.D48 1988
678'.2--dc19   88-1186
                                                    CIP
                                                    AC

Introduction

Rubber is an amazing material. It is
waterproof, stretchy, and very strong. It has
hundreds of uses. Just compare the two
pictures on the cover and on the title page!
Then look at picture [1], which illustrates a
lesser-known use of rubber.

Rubber is a natural substance from a
special type of tree discovered in the tropical
rain forests of Brazil.

In this book, I tell you the story of

[1]

Latex is the raw liquid rubber produced naturally by rubber trees.

A tapper is the worker who extracts the latex from the rubber trees. (The tapping process is described on page 10.)

Synthetic rubber is a man-made product similar to natural rubber.

rubber. In chapter 1 I tell you how seeds from rubber trees were brought from Brazil and planted in Malaysia, Indonesia, and Sri Lanka. This was the start of the rubber industry we know today. I describe the rubber tree and the milky liquid (latex) it produces. I explain how people found a way to collect the latex without damaging the tree.

In chapter 2 I describe life on a big rubber plantation. These estates are a bit like small towns, and hundreds of workers live on them. You will see how a rubber 'tapper' cuts the bark of the trees to collect the latex.

The latex has to be processed into dry rubber sheets or blocks. I explain how this is done in chapter 3. I tell you how the rubber is sold, who buys it, how the prices are set, and how the rubber is taken to the ports and loaded on to ships. These ships carry it to every corner of the world.

Early this century, scientists discovered how to make synthetic rubber. This proved essential during the Second World War (1939−45) when there was a shortage of natural rubber. I tell you a bit about synthetic rubber in chapter 4. In chapter 5, I tell you how rubber is made into all sorts of things, from aircraft tyres to the eraser you use in school.

It is an interesting story, and I hope you will enjoy reading about it.

1 · *What is rubber?*

What is the first thing that comes to your mind when you think of rubber? Car tyres, perhaps, or an eraser for rubbing out pencil marks. Or wellington boots, like those in picture [2]. You could stand in a pond all day and still have dry feet at the end of it.

Most of the world's natural rubber is produced from trees growing in South-East Asia. Yet until the latter half of the nineteenth century, rubber trees were found only in the Amazonian jungle of South America. They grew wild in the hot, humid climate, and under their bark they produced a milky substance called latex.

South American Indians had been making rubber from the latex for centuries. Christopher Columbus, the European discoverer of America, was puzzled by a strange toy he had seen in 1496. He brought back a bouncing ball made from the gum of a tree. Some rubber was imported into Europe but it was hard and difficult to work by the time it arrived. People thought it was an interesting curiosity, but not very useful. It was given its English name 'rubber' by a scientist called Joseph Priestley who noticed that it would rub out pencil marks.

In the early part of the nineteenth century ways were found to make the rubber soft so that it could be shaped. An American called Charles Goodyear found a way to prevent it melting in the heat and getting brittle in cold

[2]

[3]

weather. These discoveries made people look at rubber in a new light. They began to see how useful it could be. It was waterproof and elastic and there was no substance quite like it.

In the 1860s, two British botanists were sent to Brazil to find out more about rubber trees. They discovered that a species called *Hevea Brasiliensis* provided the best supply of latex. But the trees were dotted about in the jungle and collecting the latex was difficult and dangerous.

The British Government decided to grow rubber trees in a part of their empire which had the same climate as the Amazon rain forests. In 1870 Sir Henry Wickham brought some seeds back from Brazil. They were raised in greenhouses at Kew Gardens in London. When they were about the height of the one in picture [3], they were shipped out to Sri Lanka and Malaysia. Land was cleared in the jungle to make plantations for the new seedlings and these were the first rubber estates. They enabled rubber to be produced on a much larger scale.

What is a rubber tree like? In the wild, it lives for 100 years and grows to a height of forty metres. On the rubber plantations, the trees are kept for twenty-five years or so, and grow to a height of about twenty metres in this time. Then they are removed and replaced with newer varieties which produce more rubber.

The latex is found in a layer of tiny tubes which spiral up the tree, just underneath the bark. It consists of tiny particles of solid rubber suspended in a watery solution. Some other plants and trees contain latex, but the rubber tree produces the most. No one quite knows why it is there and what use it is to the tree.

The latex is removed by cutting through the bark and through the tubes, so that the liquid runs out. You can see someone doing this in picture [4].

Rubber from the wild trees in South America was produced by hacking into the trees with an axe. It released the latex but also ruined the tree. A new way of getting the latex out without destroying the tree was needed before the planters in South-East Asia would accept rubber as a plantation crop.

[4]

[5]

In about 1890 it was found that it was better to remove a thin strip of bark with a special knife. If the cut is made at the right angle, the knife cuts cleanly into the tubes and the latex flows out. If you look at picture [5] you will see that, just below the cut, there is a small funnel with a cup underneath. The latex flows along the cut, through the funnel, and then drops into the cup. This method is called tapping, and it is still used today. I tell you more about it in the next chapter.

Today, more than ninety per cent of the world's natural rubber is produced from trees growing in South-East Asia. More than one and a half million tonnes a year comes from Malaysia. This is thirty-six per cent of the world supply. Natural rubber also comes from Indonesia, Sri Lanka, and Thailand. About five per cent of natural rubber comes from West Africa and only about one per cent from the place where it all began, South America.

There are about seven million hectares of rubber trees in the world. That is about the size of the Republic of Ireland. Rubber is an important part of the economy to those countries which produce it. The industry provides work for hundreds of thousands of people. This huge industry started with just a few seeds gathered by one man in the jungles of South America.

2 · *The rubber plantations*

In Malaysia, about two million hectares of
land are planted with rubber trees. They are
grown on large estates called plantations or on
smallholdings. Some of the large estates are
owned by companies who need rubber, such
as tyre manufacturers. Others are privately
owned. The smallholdings are small areas of
land owned by a farmer and his family.

The estates have between 600 and 1,500
hectares of rubber trees, and are like small
towns. Each estate is run by a manager. He is
responsible for employing the workers, buying
all the equipment and materials for the estate,
planning the planting of new trees, and selling
the raw rubber.

There are between 300 and 500 workers on
a large plantation, and most of these are
tappers. There are also people who look after
the trees and plant new ones, and people who
work in the estate's processing factory. Many
of the tappers are women. Picture [6] shows a
tapper at work.

On the estate, there are houses for the
workers and their families. They are simple
houses made of wood and raised up on stilts.
This keeps them cool because the air can
circulate underneath. It also prevents flooding
during the heavy rains. The estates are often
quite a long way from the nearest town, so
each one has its own schools, shops, and
churches, temples, and mosques. There is a
doctor in case anyone is ill, and there may be

[6]

[7]

a hospital. The workers can keep their own cattle on special grazing areas on the estate.

Every tree on the estate is tapped every second day, then left for its supply of latex to build up again. The latex flows best in the coolness of the early morning.

The tappers make an early start because they must visit several hundred trees each day. They use a special knife to cut away a shaving of bark about 2 mm thick. They must do this very carefully or they will damage the tree. The cut is made at a slight angle, and spirals down either halfway or fully round the trunk. The tapper fits a cup to the tree just below the bottom of the cut. The latex flows out and down the diagonal cut into the cup.

The tapper attends to 400 or 500 trees in the same way. It takes two or three hours for all the latex to ooze out, so when she has finished tapping it is time to return to the first trees and remove the full cups. The tapper in picture [7] is pouring the contents of a cup into a collecting bucket.

The next tapping will shave away the bark below the last tapping, and so on all the way down the tree. This gives the bark a chance to heal.

The tapper takes the latex to a nearby collecting point like the one in picture [8].

The tapper's work is very skilled, and takes a long time. Sometimes the estates cannot find enough tappers to cope with all the trees. To solve this problem, automatic cutting tools are being developed.

A rubber tree cannot be tapped until it is five years old, and after twenty-five years it is

[8]

[9]

A nursery bed is a place where young plants are raised. They grow and develop strength in the sheltered conditions of the nursery before being transplanted elsewhere.

replaced. Therefore, while the tappers are at work, agricultural workers are planning for the future. There must always be a supply of trees to take the place of those which are old and exhausted.

From the beginning it was noticed that some trees gave a better supply of latex than others. Naturally the producers wanted all their trees to give a good supply. Therefore, when they planted new seeds they selected them only from the best trees. This worked quite well, but now a better method has been found. A bud is taken from a good tree and grafted on to the stem of a seedling. The bud grows into the stem to form a new plant, and the top of the original seedling is then cut off. You can see the result in picture [9]. The seedlings there are ready for planting out.

The seedlings stay in a nursery bed for the first year. They are then planted out in rows. Other crops are planted between the rows, to shade the soil and help it to retain moisture. The soil is fertilized and watered often, and the trees are kept free from pests and diseases. As the trees grow, they are thinned out so that the rows do not get too crowded. They have to be looked after carefully during these early years.

3 · *Processing the rubber*

On page 10 we left the containers of latex at a collection point. Lorries or tractors now arrive to take the latex to the processing factory.

The liquid latex straight from the tree is called 'field latex'. At the factory, most of the field latex is processed to make dry rubber. (I will tell you in a moment what happens to the rest.)

To make dry rubber, the rubber in the latex has to be 'coagulated'—this means that all the tiny particles join together to form a solid mass.

First the latex is sieved to remove any bits of dirt. Then the latex from different trees is mixed by pouring it into large tanks, and some preservative is added. This latex mixture then passes to a different tank where it is mixed with a coagulating acid. Each tank has metal separating plates which make the rubber set in thick sheets. After a few hours the sheets of rubber are taken from the tanks, and passed through rollers to squeeze out as much water as possible. The rollers give the rubber a ribbed appearance. Then they are cut into short lengths and hung up to dry, as you see in picture [10].

The final drying process takes place in a large shed filled with wood smoke. By the time it emerges the rubber has changed to a russet colour. Rubber processed in this way is called ribbed smoked sheet. You can see it in picture

[10]

[11]

[11] and it is the traditional method of preparing raw rubber.

A more modern method is to produce blocks of dry rubber. The coagulated rubber is all chopped or minced by machines. Another way is to add castor oil, which makes the rubber crumble into granules between rollers. The granules are washed and dried and then pressed into bales, like the ones in picture [12], ready for sale.

On page 13 I told you that not all the field latex was turned into dry rubber. A few products, such as rubber gloves and balloons, are made from liquid latex. Dry rubber is no good for making things like these, so about ten per cent of the field latex is sold as a liquid.

There is still far too much water in the latex. It is wasteful to ship tanks of unwanted water around the world, so the latex is made into a concentrate. First, a chemical is added to prevent it coagulating. Then it is put into a centrifugal machine, like the ones in picture [13]. These machines spin at a very high speed and throw out a lot of the water. This produces a creamy mixture containing about sixty per cent rubber.

Another method is evaporation, which dries out the unwanted water.

[12]

[13]

4 · *Life on a smallholding*

[14]

By no means all rubber is grown on great plantations. About eighty per cent of the world's rubber is grown on smallholdings. A smallholding is run in a different way from the big plantation because the farmer and his family do most of the work themselves. Many smallholding farmers have no workers at all apart from their families.

A smallholding may consist of only two or three hectares of land, containing about 1,000 rubber trees. The owner uses only part of the land to grow rubber trees. There will be a small house and a piece of land where other crops like rice, vegetables, and fruit are grown. These crops not only provide food for the family, they are a vital source of income in the early years, before the rubber trees have started to produce latex.

Some smallholdings have their own processing units: you can see a typical one in picture [14]. However, it is usually better for the farmer to take his latex to a central processing unit. This may be a cooperative, like the one in picture [15]; it processes the latex for several farmers in the area. Alternatively, it may be a factory which buys the latex from the farmer so that he does not have to worry about the processing at all. These larger units have better equipment than the individual farmers can afford, and produce a higher-quality rubber.

The smallholdings are a very important part

[15]

of the rubber industry. They produce about sixty per cent of Malaysia's raw rubber. In Indonesia and Thailand there are very few big estates, and nearly all their rubber comes from smallholdings. Unfortunately, the life is hard, and some of the farmers are very poor. They do not have enough land, and there is a long wait for the rubber trees to become productive. Trees which become exhausted cannot always be replaced promptly.

[16]

5 · *Selling the rubber*

All the world needs rubber, but it does not always want the same amount from year to year. The demand varies. There is also competition from synthetic rubber (which I tell you about in the next chapter).

More than seventy per cent of the world's natural rubber is used for making tyres. North America and Western Europe buy large amounts, and so do Russia, Eastern Europe, China, and Japan.

A buyer can order the rubber just before he needs it, or he can order it in advance. If he makes a 'firm' order in advance, the price is fixed there and then. The buyer knows he will get his rubber when he needs it, even if the market price rises for everyone else.

However, the buyer also knows that the price may have fallen by the time he gets the rubber; he would then be paying above the market rate. So he may decide to buy an 'option' instead. This means that he is given a delivery date and a price for the rubber, but he can change his mind later, and withdraw his order, if prices fall. With this method there is more risk for the producers, so an option contract is more expensive than a firm contract. The buyer has to study the world market carefully before he decides what to do.

The buyers of rubber are the manufacturing companies who will make things with the rubber and sell them. Some manufacturers buy their supplies direct from a rubber estate, but most rubber is sold through a central market. Singapore is an important trading centre for natural rubber. There are also international markets in cities such as London.

The bales of rubber are sent from the processing factories to a central market. Picture [16] shows a bale being inspected for quality. If it proves satisfactory it will be given a certificate, and a label which states the type of rubber it is and how it has been processed.

The rubber is now ready for export. In picture [17] bales of dry rubber are loaded on to a lorry. Soon it will be on its way to a port where a ship waits to take it to its destination. Liquid latex is carried to the port in road or rail tankers, and transferred to large tanker ships. Soon the rubber is on its way to the manufacturers who have ordered it.

[17]

6 · Synthetic rubber

The rubber I have told you about so far is natural rubber—the rubber which comes from trees. It needs a tropical climate to grow in, so not many countries can grow their own.

In the nineteenth century this strange material fascinated scientists in Europe and America. It would stretch and bend and keep the water out. What on earth was it made of, and why did it behave in that way?

By 1910 scientists had discovered a lot about rubber, and they knew how to make an artificial rubber from chemicals. This knowledge was not very useful at first. There was plenty of cheap natural rubber, and the synthetic version was not nearly so good. Even so, scientists kept on experimenting.

Second World War demand for rubber

During the Second World War of 1939–45 there was a huge demand for rubber. It was needed to make tyres for vehicles and aircraft. Supplies were not getting through from Asia, so an alternative had to be found. The scientists' work on synthetic rubber began to pay off. The quality had improved since the early days, and the United States began to produce synthetic rubber in large quantities.

After the war, natural rubber was available again, and for a time no one was very interested in synthetic rubber. But the companies who made it continued to improve the quality until it became a strong competitor

[18]

with natural rubber. Today, it is difficult to tell how many of the rubber articles in picture [18] are natural or synthetic.

The early scientists studied the chemical make-up of natural rubber, then looked for other chemicals which would behave in the same way. The chemicals they experimented with come from another natural

[19]

Crude oil is oil as found in its
natural state, before any
impurities have been removed, or
any refining has taken place.

substance—oil. In picture [19] you see an oil
refinery. It is here that the crude oil, which
comes out of the ground, is separated into
petrol, paraffin, and other substances. The
parts which are left are called petrochemicals.
They can be made into other things; plastics,
for example. And—as scientists discovered—
synthetic rubber.

Today, we can make more than one type of
synthetic rubber by using various mixtures of
petrochemicals. They do not produce sheets of

rubber, but liquids, which have to be processed into a latex concentrate or into dry rubber granules.

Who makes synthetic rubber and who uses it?

About half the synthetic rubber produced is made by tyre companies. Most family cars, even those used in the conditions shown in picture [20], use tyres made of a mixture of synthetic and natural rubber.

Petrochemical companies also produce synthetic rubber which they sell direct to manufacturers. An advantage to the manufacturers is that the price of the rubber does not go up and down as it does in the natural rubber market. Also the rubber can be ordered from a producer in their own country, so there are not the large transportation costs. And, of course, the producers can make as much as they need, so long as oil stocks last.

[20]

7 · Using rubber

In chapter 1 I told you that rubber was not very useful until its natural qualities had been improved. Once set hard, it could not be moulded into rubber products. It became sticky in the heat and brittle in the cold.

Two important nineteenth century inventions changed all this. First, the rubber had to be crushed to a pulp to make it soft and workable. The first 'masticator' machine to do this was invented in 1820 by an Englishman called Thomas Hancock. Today, the raw rubber is masticated in a machine called a two-roll mill, or in a huge internal mixer.

Mastication and vulcanization

A two-roll mill has rollers which turn at different speeds. As the rubber is fed through, the friction heats up the rubber and breaks up the molecules to make it soft. In an internal mixer the rubber is heated by the friction of rotors. When the rubber has been broken down, and is soft and warm, chemicals can be added to give it various properties.

In 1839 an American called Charles Goodyear discovered a process called 'vulcanization'. Mixing the masticated rubber with sulphur prevented it from becoming sticky or brittle, and made it stronger and more elastic.

Why are car tyres always black? The reason is that a substance called carbon black is added. It makes the rubber stiffer, harder, and

more resistant to abrasion.

It is during this vulcanization process that the rubber is moulded, because once it has been vulcanized it sets into the shape and cannot be re-softened. There are three ways of shaping rubber products. There are extrusion, moulding, and calendering.

Extrusion is the method used to make continuous lengths of rubber, such as the fire hoses in picture [21]. The rubber is put into an extrusion machine and is forced out through a hole the size and shape of the product being made. For hollow articles like

[22]

tubes the rubber has a central core. The rubber goes from the extrusion machine into a continuous vulcanization plant where it is vulcanized.

Many rubber articles are made by moulding. One method is called compression moulding. The mould is in two parts with a hollow shape in between. When the rubber mix has been put into the mould the two halves are pressed together, under heat.

Transfer moulding is a similar method used to make more detailed articles. The rubber is put into an outer section of the mould, then squeezed through a hole into every nook and cranny of the mould itself.

The third moulding technique is called injection moulding. This method is very fast, and is used when a lot of identical objects are required. The machine consists of a chamber containing a large screw. At one end the screw forces the rubber out through a hole and into a series of identical moulds.

Waterproofed fabrics like raincoats are made in a machine called a calender. The machine has three rollers. The rubber is forced through the first two rollers, then winds round the second roller and passes between it and the third roller. As the rubber passes through the second set of rollers, fabric is fed through as well and the rubber penetrates the fabric. It comes out as the smooth, thin sheet which you see in picture [22].

Rubber gloves, hot water bottles, elastic, and those balloons you saw on the title page—all are made from liquid latex. First the latex is mixed with certain chemicals to improve its quality and make it easier to work with. Any colouring pigments are added at this time. Latex does not have to be masticated, of course, but it does have to be vulcanized.

Articles like rubber gloves are made by a process called 'dipping'. The latex mixture is pumped into a bath. The articles are shaped on 'formers', which look like hands or hot water bottles, or whatever is being made. The

Goods made from liquid latex

27

[23] formers are first dipped into a liquid which prepares their surface to take the latex. Then they are dipped into the latex, and—covered with their skin of latex—are dried and vulcanized in temperatures of approximately 100°C.

Elastic thread is made by extrusion. The latex is forced out of the machine, through very fine holes, straight into an acid bath where it coagulates. The thread is washed and passed through a heated tunnel where it dries and vulcanizes. It is covered in talc to prevent it sticking to itself, and wound on to spools.

Latex is also used to make the foam which is used in furniture and as carpet backing. After being whipped up into a frothy mixture, it is dried and vulcanized with the air bubbles trapped in it. Some foam rubber products are made by pouring the foam into a mould and letting it set. Carpet backings are made by covering the carpet with foam to which vulcanizing chemicals have been added, which make it set.

The hundreds of uses for rubber

Tyres, including those huge tractor tyres in picture [23], are made by a combination of moulding and calendering. The toughest types, such as those for aircraft and heavy lorries, are made entirely from natural rubber because less heat will build up during use than with synthetic rubber. Other car tyres are normally made from a mixture of synthetic and natural rubber. The different parts of the tyre are made separately, then put together before the final moulding and vulcanization.

The car trade uses rubber in other ways, too. Windscreen wiper blades are made by injection moulding. There are rubber hoses made by extrusion, and mats made by compression moulding. Then there are all sorts of small springs which cut down on

[24]

vibration and make the car more comfortable.

The soles of the shoes in picture [24] may be made of moulded rubber. The flooring of public places like airports or railway stations are often made of rubber. Carpets in homes and offices are often backed with foam rubber. The conveyor belts used in industry, in coal mines, and at airports, are made of rubber or a mixture of rubber and fabric. Bridges and buildings are sometimes mounted on rubber blocks to prevent vibration. Sports equipment often contains some rubber.

These are just some of the uses of rubber. I am sure you can find others. Hundreds of everyday objects have at least some rubber parts. The whole world has grown amazingly dependent on rubber since those seeds were brought out of Brazil, little more than a century ago.

Index

Acknowledgements for photographs: BP Chemicals 19; BTR Silvertown 2, 22; Jacqueline Dineen, title page; Dunlop Hiflex 21; Ford Motor Company, cover, 20; GKN Sankey 24; The Malaysian Rubber Producers' Research Association, picture on contents page and nos. 3, 4, 5, 6, 7, 8, 9, 10, 11, 12, 13, 14, 15, 16, 17, 18, 23; United Kingdom Atomic Energy Authority 1.